The Poetry of Bliss Carman

Volume XVII - Echoes From Vagabondia

Co-Authored with Richard Hovey

William Bliss Carman was born in Fredericton, in New Brunswick on April 15th 1861. He was educated at Fredericton Collegiate School before moving to the University of New Brunswick, obtaining his B.A. there in 1881. As is common with so many writers his first published piece was for the University magazine and for Carman that was in 1879.

After several years editing various magazines and periodicals Carman first published a poetry volume in 1893 with Low Tide on Grand Pré. There was no Canadian company prepared to publish and when an American company did so it went bankrupt.

The following year was decidedly better. His partnership with the American poet Richard Hovey had given birth to Songs of Vagabondia. It was an immediate success.

That success prompted the Boston firm, Stone & Kimball, to reissue Low Tide on Grand Pré and to hire Carman as the editor of its literary journal, The Chapbook.

Carman brought out, in 1895, Behind the Arras, a somewhat more serious and philosophical work centered on the premise of a long meditation, using the speaker's house and its many rooms, as a symbol of life and the choices to be made.

In 1896 Carman met Mrs Mary Perry King, who rapidly became patron, adviser and sometime lover. She also became his writing collaborator on two verse dramas.

In 1897 Carman published Ballad of Lost Haven, and in 1898, By the Aurelian Wall, the title poem itself was an elegy to John Keats and the book was a collection of formal elegies.

As the century turned Carman was hard at work on a five-volume set of poetry "Pans Pipes". The excellence of a number of these poems did much to install Carman as the most noted of Canadian Poets and eventually their own Poet Laureate.

In 1912 the final work in the Vagabondia series was published. Richard Hovey had died in 1900 and so this last work was purely Carman's. It has a distinct elegiac tone as if remembering the past works themselves.

On October 28th, 1921 Carman was honored by the newly-formed Canadian Authors' Association where he was crowned Canada's Poet Laureate with a wreath of maple leaves.

William Bliss Carman died of a brain hemorrhage at the age of 68 in New Canaan on the 8th June, 1929.

Index of Contents

SPRING'S SARABAND

Over the hills of April
With soft winds hand in hand,
Impassionate and dreamy-eyed,
Spring leads her saraband.
Her garments float and gather
And swirl along the plain,
Her headgear is the golden sun,
Her cloak the silver rain.

With color and with music,
With perfumes and with pomp,
By meadowland and upland,
Through pasture, wood, and swamp,
With promise and enchantment
Leading her mystic mime,
She comes to lure the world anew
With joy as old as time.

Quick lifts the marshy chorus
To transport, trill on trill;
There 's not a rod of stony ground
Unanswering on the hill.
The brooks and little rivers
Dance down their wild ravines,
And children in the city squares
Keep time, to tambourines.

The bluebird in the orchard
Is lyrical for her,
The starling with his meadow pipe
Sets all the wood astir,
The hooded white spring-beauties
Are curtsying in the breeze,
The blue hepaticas are out
Under the chestnut trees.

The maple buds make glamor,
Viburnum waves its bloom,
The daffodils and tulips
Are risen from the tomb.
The lances of Narcissus
Have pierced the wintry mold;
The commonplace seems paradise
Through veils of greening gold.

O heart, hear thou the summons,

Put every grief away,
When all the motley masques of earth
Are glad upon a day.
Alack, that any mortal
Should less than gladness bring
Into the choral joy that sounds
The saraband of spring!

THE FLUTE OF SPRING

I know a shining meadow stream
That winds beneath an Eastern hill,
And all year long in sun or gloom
Its murmuring voice is never still.

The summer dies more gently there,
The April flowers are earlier, —
The first warm rain-wind from the Sound
Sets all their eager hearts astir.

And there when lengthening twilights fall
As softly as a wild bird's wing,
Across the valley in the dusk
I hear the silver flute of spring.

DAFFODIL'S RETURN

What matter if the sun be lost?
What matter though the sky be gray?
There 's joy enough about the house,
For Daffodil comes home to-day.

There 's news of swallows on the air,
There 's word of April on the way,
They 're calling flowers within the street,
And Daffodil comes home to-day.

O who would care what fate may bring,
Or what the years may take away!
There 's life enough within the hour,
For Daffodil comes home to-day.

THE URBAN PAN

Once more the magic days are come
With stronger sun and milder air;
The shops are full of daffodils;
There 's golden leisure everywhere.
I heard my Lou this morning shout:
"Here comes the hurdy-gurdy man!"
And through the open window caught
The piping of the urban Pan.

I laid my wintry task aside,
And took a day to follow joy:
The trail of beauty and the call
That lured me when I was a boy.
I looked, and there looked up at me
A smiling, swarthy, hairy man
With kindling eye — and well I knew
The piping of the urban Pan.

He caught my mood; his hat was off;
I tossed the ungrudged silver down.
The cunning vagrant, every year
He casts his spell upon the town!
And we must fling him, old and young,
Our dimes or coppers, as we can;
And every heart must leap to hear
The piping of the urban Pan.

The music swells and fades again,
And I in dreams am far away,
Where a bright river sparkles down
To meet a blue Aegean bay.
There, in the springtime of the world,
Are dancing fauns, and in their van,
Is one who pipes a deathless tone —
The earth-born and the urban Pan.

And so he follows down the block,
A troop of children in his train,
The light-foot dancers of the street
Enamored of the reedy strain.
I hear their laughter rise and ring
Above the noise of truck and van,
As down the mellow wind fades out
The piping of the urban Pan.

THE SAILING OF THE FLEETS

Now the spring is in the town,
Now the wind is in the tree,
And the wintered keels go down
To the calling of the sea.

Out from mooring, dock, and slip,
Through the harbor buoys they glide,
Drawing seaward till they dip
To the swirling of the tide.

One by one and two by two,
Down the channel turns they go,
Steering for the open blue
Where the salty great airs blow;

Craft of many a build and trim,
Every stitch of sail unfurled,
Till they hang upon the rim
Of the azure ocean world.

Who has ever, man or boy,
Seen the sea all flecked with gold,
And not longed to go with joy
Forth upon adventures bold?

Who could bear to stay indoor,
Now the wind is in the street,
For the creaking of the oar
And the tugging of the sheet!

Now the spring is in the town,
Who would not a rover be,
When the wintered keels go down
To the calling of the sea?

THE LAST DAY AT STORMFIELD

At Redding, Connecticut,
The April sunrise pours
Over the hardwood ridges
Softening and greening now
In the first magic of spring.

The wild cherry trees are in bloom,
The bloodroot is white underfoot,
The serene early light flows on,
Touching with glory the world,
And flooding the large upper room
Where a sick man sleeps.
Slowly he opens his eyes,
After long weariness, smiles,
And stretches his arms overhead,
While those about him take heart.

With his awakening strength
(Morning and spring in the air,
The strong clean scents of earth,
The call of the golden-shaft
Ringing across the hills),
He takes up his heartening book,
Opens the volume and reads, —
A page of old rugged Carlyle,
The dour philosopher
Who looked askance upon life,
Lurid, ironical, grim,
Yet sound at the core.

But weariness returns;
He lays the book aside
With his glasses upon the bed,
And gladly sleeps. Sleep,
Blessed abundant sleep,
Is all that he needs.

And when the close of day
Reddens upon the hills
And washes the room with rose,
In the twilight hush
The Summoner comes to him
Ever so gently, unseen,
Touches him on the shoulder;
And with the departing sun
Our great funning friend is gone.

How he has made us laugh!
A whole generation of men
Smiled in the joy of his wit.
But who knows whether he was not
Like those deep jesters of old
Who dwelt at the courts of kings,
Arthur's, Pendragon's, Lear's,

Plying the wise fool's trade,
Making men merry at will,
Hiding their deeper thoughts
Under a motley array, —
Keen-eyed, serious men,
Watching the sorry world,
The gaudy pageant of life,
With pity and wisdom and love

Fearless, extravagant, wild,
His caustic merciless mirth
Was leveled at pompous shams.
Doubt not behind that mask
There dwelt the soul of a man,
Resolute, sorrowing, sage,
As sure a champion of good
As ever rode forth to fray.

Haply — who knows? — somewhere
In Avalon, Isle of Dreams,
In vast contentment at last,
With every grief done away,
While Chaucer and Shakespeare wait,
And Molière hangs on his words,
And Cervantes not far off
Listens and smiles apart,
With that incomparable drawl
He is jesting with Dagonet now.

THE SHIPS OF YULE

When I was just a little boy,
Before I went to school,
I had a fleet of forty sail
I called the Ships of Yule;

Of every rig, from rakish brig
And gallant barkentine,
To little Fundy fishing boats
With gunwales painted green.

They used to go on trading trips
Around the world for me,
For though I had to stay on shore
My heart was on the sea.

They stopped at every port of call
From Babylon to Rome,
To load with all the lovely things
We never had at home;

With elephants and ivory
Bought from the King of Tyre,
And shells and silk and sandal-wood
That sailor men admire;

With figs and dates from Samarcand,
And squatty ginger-jars,
And scented silver amulets
From Indian bazaars;

With sugar-cane from Port of Spain,
And monkeys from Ceylon,
And paper lanterns from Pekin
With painted dragons on;

With cocoanuts from Zanzibar,
And pines from Singapore;
And when they had unloaded these
They could go back for more.

And even after I was big
And had to go to school,
My mind was often far away
Aboard the Ships of Yule.

IN ST. GERMAIN STREET

Through the street of St. Germain
March the tattered hosts of rain,

While the wind with vagrant fife
Whips their chilly ranks to life.

From the window I can see
Their ghostly banners blowing free,

As they pass to where the ships
Crowd about the wharves and slips.

There at day's end they embark
To invade the realms of dark,

And the sun comes out again
In the street of St. Germain.

IN ST. CECILIA STREET

Each morning when I hear the chimes
Of heavenly St. Cecilia's ringing,
I think if I get up betimes
I, too, might hear the angels singing.

Then up I jump, with such a start
That I am dressed before I know it,
And such a gladness in my heart,
I 'm sure all day my face must show it.

'SCONSET

Did you ever hear of 'Sconset, where there 's nothing much but moors,
And beach and sea and silence and eternal out-of-doors —
Where the azure round of ocean meets the paler dome of day,
Where the sailing clouds of summer on the sea-line melt away,
And there 's not an ounce of trouble
Anywhere?

Where the field-larks in the morning will be crying at the door,
With the whisper of the moor-wind and the surf along the shore;
Where the little shingled houses down the little grassy street
Are gray with salt of sea-winds, and the strong sea-air is sweet
With the flowers in their door-yards;
Me for there!

THE PATH TO SANKOTY

It winds along the headlands
Above the open sea —
The lonely moorland footpath
That leads to Sankoty.

The crooning sea spreads sailless
And gray to the world's rim,
Where hang the reeking fog-banks

Primordial and dim.

There fret the ceaseless currents,
And the eternal tide
Chafes over hidden shallows
Where the white horses ride.

The wistful fragrant moorlands
Whose smile bids panic cease,
Lie treeless and cloud-shadowed
In grave and lonely peace.

Across their flowering bosom,
From the far end of day
Blow clean the great soft moor-winds
All sweet with rose and bay.

A world as large and simple
As first emerged for man,
Cleared for the human drama,
Before the play began.

O well the soul must treasure
The calm that sets it free —
The vast and tender skyline,
The sea-turn's wizardry,

Solace of swaying grasses,
The friendship of sweet-fern —
And in the world's confusion
Remembering, must yearn

To tread the moorland footpath
That leads to Sankoty,
Hearing the field-larks shrilling
Beside the sailless sea.

THE CRY OF THE HILLBORN

I am homesick for the mountains —
My heroic mother hills —
And the longing that is on me
No solace ever stills.

I would climb to brooding summits
With their old untarnished dreams,

Cool my heart in forest shadows
To the lull of falling streams;

Hear the innocence of aspens
That babble in the breeze,
And the fragrant sudden showers
That patter on the trees.

I am lonely for my thrushes
In their hermitage withdrawn,
Toning the quiet transports
Of twilight and of dawn.

I need the pure, strong mornings,
When the soul of day is still,
With the touch of frost that kindles
The scarlet on the hill;

Lone trails and winding woodroads
To outlooks wild and high,
And the pale moon waiting sundown
Where ledges cut the sky.

I dream of upland clearings
Where cones of sumac burn,
And gaunt and gray-mossed boulders
Lie deep in beds of fern;

The gray and mottled beeches,
The birches' satin sheen,
The majesty of hemlocks
Crowning the blue ravine.

My eyes dim for the skyline
Where purple peaks aspire,
And the forges of the sunset
Flare up in golden fire.

There crests look down unheeding
And see the great winds blow,
Tossing the huddled tree-tops
In gorges far below;

Where cloud-mists from the warm earth
Roll up about their knees,
And hang their filmy tatters
Like prayers upon the trees.

I cry for night-blue shadows
On plain and hill and dome, —
The spell of old enchantments,
The sorcery of home.

MORNING IN THE HILLS

How quiet is the morning in the hills!
The stealthy shadows of the summer clouds
Trail through the cañon, and the mountain stream
Sounds his sonorous music far below
In the deep-wooded wind-enchanted clove.

Hemlock and aspen, chestnut, beech, and fir
Go tiering down from storm-worn crest and ledge,
While in the hollows of the dark ravine
See the red road emerge, then disappear
Towards the wide plain and fertile valley lands.

My forest cabin half-way up the glen
Is solitary, save for one wise thrush,
The sound of falling water, and the wind
Mysteriously conversing with the leaves.

Here I abide unvisited by doubt,
Dreaming of far-off turmoil and despair,
The race of men and love and fleeting time,
What life may be, or beauty, caught and held
For a brief moment at eternal poise.

What impulse now shall quicken and make live
This outward semblance and this inward self?
One breath of being fills the bubble world,
Colored and frail, with fleeting change on change.

Surely some God contrived so fair a thing
In the vast leisure of uncounted days,
And touched it with the breath of living joy,
Wondrous and fair and wise! It must be so.

PAN IN THE CATSKILLS

They say that he is dead, and now no more
The reedy syrinx sounds among the hills,

When the long summer heat is on the land.
But I have heard the Catskill thrushes sing,
And therefore am incredulous of death,
Of pain and sorrow and mortality.

In those blue cañons, deep with hemlock shade,
In solitudes of twilight or of dawn,
I have been rapt away from time and care
By the enchantment of a golden strain
As pure as ever pierced the Thracian wild,
Filling the listener with a mute surmise.

At evening and at morning I have gone
Down the cool trail between the beech-tree boles,
And heard the haunting music of the wood
Ring through the silence of the dark ravine,
Flooding the earth with beauty and with joy
And all the ardors of creation old.

And then within my pagan heart awoke
Remembrance of far-off and fabled years
In the untarnished sunrise of the world,
When clear-eyed Hellas in her rapture heard
A slow mysterious piping wild and keen
Thrill through her vales, and whispered, "It is Pan!"

THE DREAMERS

Charlemagne with knight and lord,
In the hill at Ingelheim,
Slumbers at the council board,
Seated waiting for the time.

With their swords across their knees
In that chamber dimly lit,
Chin on breast like effigies
Of the dreaming gods, they sit.

Long ago they went to sleep,
While great wars above them hurled,
Taking counsel how to keep
Giant evil from the world.

Golden-armored, iron-crowned,
There in silence they await
The last war, — in war renowned,

Done with doubting and debate.

What is all our clamor for?
Petty virtue, puny crime,
Beat in vain against the door
Of the hill at Ingelheim.

When at last shall dawn the day
For the saving of the world,
They will forth in war array,
Iron-armored, golden-curled.

In the hill at Ingelheim,
Still, they say, the Emperor,
Like a warrior in his prime,
Waits the message at the door.

Shall the long enduring fight
Break above our heads in vain,
Plunged in lethargy and night,
Like the men of Charlemagne?

Comrades, through the Council Hall
Of the heart, inert and dumb,
Hear ye not the summoning call,
"Up, my lords, the hour is come!"

THE COUNCILLORS

In the purple heat haze
Of long midsummer days
Lay the range, peak on peak,
Till one thought, "Could they speak,
Those old ones who heard
The first life-bringing word!"

With the primal unrest
Locked away in their breast,
Unperturbed they await
The fulfilment of fate,
Seated there on the plain,
Like King Charlemagne
And his heroes who keep
The long council of sleep,
Until need and the hour
Shall recall them to power.

Once an age the King wakes.
"Is it time?" his voice breaks
The silence. "Nay, Sire."
Then the echoes retire,
And sleep falls again
Gray and softer than rain.

Thus Mount Holyoke
Overheard, as he woke,
The yearn and the sigh,
Between Low and High, —

Toby speaking to Tom,
"Thy distance of blue
I can hardly see through,
Proclaims the old story
Of possible glory,
The entrancement of rapture
Our utmost may capture,
Adventuring still
Led by vision and will, —
Thou truth's Chrysostom!
Thy beauty and glamor
Above the world's clamor
Are aglow with a thought
Urgent, mystic, untaught,
Neither Christian nor Rom,
Of escape and of flight
To the spirit's lone height,
Beyond the last verge
Of soul's strife and surge,
The dominion past dream,
Where accord is supreme.
Undespairing and bold,
Through what cycles untold
Of calm, storm, sun and rain,
Soared thy life to attain
Its transcendence serene, —
That victorious mien
Over travail's maelstrom!"

Then Tom said to Toby,
"In the farness divine
Each hue, every line,
Must inblend and suspire
With the tone of desire,
Till all flaws be recast

To perfection at last.
Whether lofty or low be
Thy measure, what matters?
When blinding noon scatters,
And soul grows aware
Of a soul through the glare,
Convinced there must so be
A reach and a lift
Through the dusk's purple rift,
To the large, fair, and new
Where ideals come true,
With no doubt of the end,
Let heart hold its trend.
Shall Potumcook disdain
The deep corn-bearing plain,
Through the slow-plowing years?
Thou art crowned with thy peers,
When over thy crest
The great sun from the West
Bids the glory and glow be."

Then said Holyoke,
"It is well that you spoke.
Low and High are as one,
When soul's service is done!"

Peak on peak lay the range,
With no word to exchange,
Not a hint to break through
That soft stillness of blue, —
All as silent as when
God first whispered to men.

There like the great king
With his captains a-ring,
These councillors sleep.
Untroubled and deep
Is their rest. They abide
Heat and cold, time and tide;
Their supreme heritage,
To grow lovely with age.
How could they but dream true,
With their heads in the blue,
And their feet in the flow
Of the river where go
Mirrored stories of time?
While the world, out of chime
And unheeding, goes by,

They translate earth and sky,
These old mystics. Ah, theirs
Are eternal affairs!

A CONUNDRUM

I am Greek in the morning
And Gothic at night;
I change without warning
From grief to delight.

I 'm grim in November,
I 'm gaudy in June,
As warm as an ember,
As cold as the moon.

I 'm sober on Sunday,
On Monday I 'm blue;
But what I do one day
I don't always do.

I 'm Western in bearing,
And Eastern in breed,
The Occident's daring,
The Orient's creed.

I camp or I travel,
I triumph or fail,
And who shall unravel
The loops of my trail?

The dust of the desert,
The wind of the sea,
The spray of the river
Are mingled in me.

I run the whole gamut
From heaven to hell,
And when I don't damn it,
I say it is well.

APOLOGIA

Call him a son of fantastical fortune,

With songs of elation and sighs of despair;
Say he was careless, impatient, and moody,
Fickle as water and wilful as air;

Say he would idle, procrastinate, dally,
Spend golden days without doing a thing,
Plan while his fellows made much of the present,
Smile as the opportune hour took wing;

Aware of ambition, perfection, and power,
Yet willing to loiter and let the world be;
Say there was never a reed in the river
More ready to bend to the current than he;

Say he could never refuse a companion
Bidding him in from the street to the bar,
Never resist the enchantment of pleasure —
Joy was his captain and beauty his star;

Call him a ne'er-do-well, harlequin, dreamer,
Flash of the rocket and froth of the sea;
Say his whole life was a waste of endeavor —
Never a moment unloving of thee!

Revel of April, or ravage of winter,
What cares the mountain, broad based as the world?
Are the deeps of the ocean disturbed by the turmoil,
When tempests are loosed and tornadoes unfurled?

Nay, is the mighty sun darkened in heaven
Every time earth must revolve into night?
Do the stars wheel to a faltering measure?
Shall not the morning return to the height?

So, thou dear heart, beyond folly or failure,
Undimmed by distraction, by doubt undismayed,
The soul of a man with the calm of an angel
Abides in the heaven thy friendship has made.

A COLOPHON

When all my writing has been done
Except the final colophon,

And I must bid beloved verse
Farewell for better or for worse,

Let me not linger o'er the page
In doubting and regretful age;

But as an unknown scribe in some
Monastic dim scriptorium,

When twilight on his labor fell
At the glad-heard refection bell,

Might add poor Body's thanks to be
From spiritual toils set free,

Let me conclude with hearty zest, —
Laus Deo! Nunc bibendum est!

ON THE PLAZA

One August day I sat beside
A café window open wide
To let the shower-freshened air
Blow in across the Plaza, where
In golden pomp against the dark
Green leafy background of the Park,
St. Gaudens' hero, gaunt and grim,
Rides on with Victory leading him.

The wet, black asphalt seemed to hold
In every hollow pools of gold,
And clouds of gold and pink and gray
Were piled up at the end of day,
Far down the cross street, where one tower
Still glistened from the drenching shower.

A weary white-haired man went by,
Cooling his forehead gratefully
After the day's great heat. A girl,
Her thin white garments in a swirl
Blown back against her breasts and knees,
Like a Winged Victory in the breeze,
Alive and modern and superb,
Crossed from the circle to the curb.

We sat there watching people pass,
Clinking the ice against the glass
And talking idly — books or art,

Or something equally apart
From the essential stress and strife
That rudely form and further life,
Glad of a respite from the heat,
When down the middle of the street,
Trundling a hurdy-gurdy, gay
In spite of the dull-stifling day,
Three street-musicians came. The man,
With hair and beard as black as Pan,
Strolled on one side with lordly grace,
While a young girl tugged at a trace
Upon the other. And between
The shafts there walked a laughing queen,
Bright as a poppy, strong and free.
What likelier land than Italy
Breeds such abandon? Confident
And rapturous in mere living spent
Each moment to the utmost, there
With broad, deep chest and kerchiefed hair,
With head thrown back, bare throat, and waist
Supple, heroic and free-laced,
Between her two companions walked
This splendid woman, chaffed and talked,
Did half the work, made all the cheer
Of that small company.

No fear
Of failure in a soul like hers
That every moment throbs and stirs
With merry ardor, virile hope,
Brave effort, nor in all its scope
Has room for thought or discontent,
Each day its own sufficient vent
And source of happiness.

Without
A trace of bitterness or doubt
Of life's true worth, she strode at ease
Before those empty palaces,
A simple heiress of the earth
And all its joys by happy birth,
Beneficent as breeze or dew,
And fresh as though the world were new
And toil and grief were not. How rare
A personality was there!

DUST OF THE STREET

This cosmic dust beneath our feet
Rising to hurry down the street,

Borne by the wind and blown astray
In its erratic senseless way,

Is the same stuff as you and I —
With knowledge and desire put by.

Thousands of times since time began
It has been used for making man,

Freighted like us with every sense
Of spirit and intelligence,

To walk the world and know the fine
Large consciousness of things divine.

These wandering atoms in their day
Perhaps have passed this very way,

With eager step and flowerlike face,
With lovely ardor, poise, and grace,

On what delightful errands bent,
Passionate, generous, and intent, —

An angel still, though veiled and gloved,
Made to love us and to be loved.

Friends, when the summons comes for me
To turn my back (reluctantly)

On this delightful play, I claim
Only one thing in friendship's name;

And you will not decline a task
So slight, when it is all I ask:

Scatter my ashes in the street
Where avenue and crossway meet.

I beg you of your charity,
No granite and cement for me,

To needlessly perpetuate

An unimportant name and date.

Others may wish to lay them down
On some fair hillside far from town,

Where slim white birches wave and gleam
Beside a shadowy woodland stream,

Or in luxurious beds of fern,
But I would have my dust return

To the one place it loved the best
In days when it was happiest.

BRONSON HOWARD

Others must praise him for the plays he wrote,
Or criticise him in perfunctory mode.
I only know our peerless friend is gone,
Leaving for us an emptier world where once
This gentlest of all gentlemen abode.

Let us not wrong so genuine a soul —
So modest after all his honored years —
With high-flown eulogy and sounding phrase.
It is enough that loss of him must reach
To the profound sincerity of tears.

Many will see him still with dog and pipe
Strolling through little 'Sconset by the sea,
Among the happy bathers on the beach,
Watching the sunset on the purple moors,
Or on the way to lonely Sankoty.

The courtly welcome from his cabin door,
Far from the mainland on his isle of dreams,
Must hold its spell forever in our hearts,
To shame ungenerous credence or offense
With faith in simple kindness and high themes.

When last I saw him it was at his ease
On the wide lounge before the blazing fire —
The hospitable hearthstone of The Players.
So free of spirit, so fine, and so humane,
Kindly to judge and kindling to inspire!

Dear Bronson Howard! Could mortal ever live
More loyally for loveliness and right?
We shall not find him now by hearth nor shore,
But all life long love must recall his smile —
Immortal friend of sweetness and of light.

TO A FRIEND

Dear friend, our comrade who left here
His beautiful unfinished songs,
With Shelley and the sons of light
To the majestic past belongs.

By winter fire, by summer sun,
We shall not have him any more.
That courtly leisure, that slow smile,
Have found new countries to explore.

He cannot lift you hand nor voice,
In the old way to let you know
He loves you and would have you glad
He uses mine to tell you so.

TO A YOUNG LADY ON HER BIRTHDAY

The marching years go by,
And brush your garment's hem.
The bandits by and by
Will bid you go with them.

Trust not that caravan!
Old vagabonds are they;
They 'll rob you if they can,
And make believe it 's play.

Make the old robbers give
Of all the spoils they bear, —
Their truth, to help you live, —
Their joy, to keep you fair.

Ask not for gauds nor gold,
Nor fame that falsely rings;
The foolish world grows old
Caring for all these things.

Make all your sweet demands
For happiness alone,
And the years will fill your hands
With treasures rarely known.

THE ANGEL OF JOY

There is no grief for me
Nor sadness any more;
For since I first knew thee
Great Joy has kept my door.

That angel of the calm
All-comprehending smile,
No menace can dismay,
No falsity beguile.

Out of the house of life
Before him fled away
Languor, regret, and strife
And sorrow on that day.

Grim fear, unmanly doubt,
And impotent despair
Went at his bidding forth
Among the things that were, —

Leaving a place all clean,
Resounding of the sea
And decked with forest green,
To be a home for thee.

A LYRIC

Oh, once I could not understand
The sob within the throat of spring, —
The shrilling of the frogs, nor why
The birds so passionately sing.

That was before your beauty came
And stooped to teach my soul desire,
When on these mortal lips you laid
The magic and immortal fire.

I wondered why the sea should seem
So gray, so lonely, and so old;
The sigh of level-driving snows
In winter so forlornly cold.

I wondered what it was could give
The scarlet autumn pomps their pride,
And paint with colors not of earth
The glory of the mountainside.

I could not tell why youth should dream
And worship at the evening star,
And yet must go with eager feet
Where danger and where splendor are.

I could not guess why men at times,
Beholding beauty, should go mad
With joy or sorrow or despair
Or some unknown delight they had.

I wondered what they would receive
From Time's inexorable hand
So full of loveliness and doom.
But now, ah, now I understand!

A WOOD-PATH

At evening and at morning
By an enchanted way
I walk the world in wonder,
And have no word to say.

It is the path we traversed
One twilight, thou and I;
Thy beauty all a rapture,
My spirit all a cry.

The red leaves fall upon it,
The moon and mist and rain,
But not the magic footfall
That made its meaning plain.

NIKE

What do men give thanks for?
I give thanks for one,
Lovelier than morning,
Dearer than the sun.

Such a head the victors
Must have praised and known,
With that breast and bearing,
Nike's very own —

As superb, untrammeled,
Rhythmed and poised and free
As the strong pure sea-wind
Walking on the sea;

Such a hand as Beauty
Uses with full heart,
Seeking for her freedom
In new shapes of art;

Soft as rain in April,
Quiet as the days
Of the purple asters
And the autumn haze;

With a soul more subtle
Than the light of stars,
Frailer than a moth's wing
To the touch that mars;

Wise with all the silence
Of the waiting hills,
When the gracious twilight
Wakes in them and thrills;

With a voice more tender
Than the early moon
Hears among the thrushes
In the woods of June;

Delicate as grasses
When they lift and stir —
One-sweet lyric woman —
I give thanks for her.

My tent stands in a garden
Of aster and goldenrod,
Tilled by the rain and the sunshine,
And sown by the hand of God, —
An old New England pasture
Abandoned to peace and time,
And by the magic of beauty
Reclaimed to the sublime.

About it are golden woodlands
Of tulip and hickory;
On the open ridge behind it
You may mount to a glimpse of sea, —
The far-off, blue, Homeric
Rim of the world's great shield,
A border of boundless glamor
For the soul's familiar field.

In purple and gray-wrought lichen
The boulders lie in the sun;
Along its grassy footpath
The white-tailed rabbits run.
The crickets work and chirrup
Through the still afternoon;
And the owl calls from the hillside
Under the frosty moon.

The odorous wild grape clambers
Over the tumbling wall,
And through the autumnal quiet
The chestnuts open and fall.
Sharing time's freshness and fragrance,
Part of the earth's great soul,
Here man's spirit may ripen
To wisdom serene and whole.

Shall we not grow with the asters —
Never reluctant nor sad,
Not counting the cost of being,
Living to dare and be glad?
Shall we not lift with the crickets
A chorus of ready cheer,
Braving the frost of oblivion,
Quick to be happy here?

Is my will as sweet as the wild grape,

Spreading delight on the air
For the passer-by's enchantment,
Subtle and unaware?
Have I as brave a spirit,
Sprung from the self-same mould,
As this weed from its own contentment
Lifting its shaft of gold?

The deep red cones of the sumach
And the woodbine's crimson's sprays
Have bannered the common roadside
For the pageant of passing days.
These are the oracles Nature
Fills with her holy breath,
Giving them glory of color,
Transcending the shadow of death.

Here in the sifted sunlight
A spirit seems to brood
On the beauty and worth of being,
In tranquil, instinctive mood;
And the heart, filled full of gladness
Such as the wise earth knows,
Wells with a full thanksgiving
For the gifts that life bestows:

For the ancient and virile nurture
Of the teeming primordial ground,
For the splendid gospel of color,
The rapt revelations of sound;
For the morning-blue above us
And the rusted gold of the fern,
For the chickadee's call to valor
Bidding the faint-heart turn;

For fire and running water,
Snowfall and summer rain;
For sunsets and quiet meadows,
The fruit and the standing grain;
For the solemn hour of moonrise
Over the crest of trees,
When the mellow lights are kindled
In the lamps of the centuries;

For those who wrought aforetime,
Led by the mystic strain
To strive for the larger freedom,
And live for the greater gain;

For plenty and peace and playtime,
The homely goods of earth,
And for rare immaterial treasures
Accounted of little worth;

For art and learning and friendship,
Where beneficent truth is supreme, —
Those everlasting cities
Built on the hills of dream;
For all things growing and goodly
That foster this life, and breed
The immortal flower of wisdom
Out of the mortal seed.

But most of all for the spirit
That cannot rest nor bide
In stale and sterile convenience,
Nor safely proven and tried,
But still inspired and driven,
Must seek what better may be,
And up from the loveliest garden
Must climb for a glimpse of sea.

TE DEUM

If I could paint you the autumn color, the melting glow upon all things laid,
The violet haze of Indian summer, before its splendor begins to fade,
When scarlet has reached its breathless moment, and gold the hush of its glory now,
That were a mightier craft than Titian's, the heart to lift and the head to bow.

I should be lord of a world of rapture, master of magic and gladness, too, —
The touch of wonder transcending science, the solace escaping from line and hue;
I would reveal through tint and texture the very soul of this earth of ours,
Forever yearning through boundless beauty to exalt the spirit with all her powers.

See where it lies by the lake this morning, our autumn hillside of hardwood trees,
A masterpiece of the mighty painter who works in the primal mysteries.
A living tapestry, rich and glowing with blended marvels, vermilion and dun,
Hung out for the pageant of time that passes along an avenue of the sun!

The crown of the ash is tinged with purple, the hickory leaves are Etruscan gold,
And the tulip-tree lifts yellow banners against the blue for a signal bold;
The oaks in crimson cohorts stand, a myriad sumack torches mass
In festal pomp and victorious pride, when the vision of spring is brought to pass.

Down from the line of the shore's deep shadows another and softer picture lies,

As if the soul of the lake in slumber should harbor a dream of paradise, —
Passive and blurred and unsubstantial, lulling the sense and luring the mind
With the spell of an empty fairy world, where sinew and sap are left behind.

So men dream of a far-off heaven of power and knowledge and endless joy,
Asleep to the moment's fine elation, dull to the day's divine employ,
Musing over a phantom image, born of fantastic hope and fear,
Of the very happiness life engenders and earth provides — our privilege here.

Dare we dispel a single transport, neglect the worth that is here and now,
Yet dream of enjoying its shadowy semblance in the by-and-by somewhere, somehow?
I heard the wind on the hillside whisper, "They ill prepare for a journey hence
Who waste the senses and starve the spirit in a world all made for spirit and sense.

"Is the full stream fed from a stifled source, or the ripe fruit filled from a blighted flower?
Are not the brook and the blossom greatened through many a busy beatified hour?
Not in the shadow but in the substance, plastic and potent at our command,
Are all the wisdom and gladness of heart; this is the kingdom of heaven at hand."

So I will pass through the lovely world, and partake of beauty to feed my soul.
With earth my domain and growth my portion, how should I sue for a further dole?
In the lift I feel of immortal rapture, in the flying glimpse I gain of truth,
Released is the passion that sought perfection, assuaged the ardor of dreamful youth.

The patience of time shall teach me courage, the strength of the sun shall lend me poise.
I would give thanks for the autumn glory, for the teaching of earth and all her joys.
Her fine fruition shall well suffice me; the air shall stir in my veins like wine;
While the moment waits and the wonder deepens, my life shall merge with the life divine.

ON BURIAL HILL

While the slow-filtered sorcery
Of Indian summer lay
Upon the golden-shadowed streets
Of Concord yesterday,
We climbed the rocky path that led
Through hallowed air all still,
Where Concord men first laid their dead
To rest on Burial Hill.

Her sages and her poets lie
In Sleepy Hollow ground;
But here, unvisited, apart,
Her good men unrenowned, —
Those vanished folk who greatly did,
Because they greatly planned.

Here in the slanting mellow sun
Their sinking headstones stand.

Close to the stone-walled village street
It rises in deep shade, —
This cherished place about whose base
Their first homesteads were made.
Here the first smoke rose from the hearth
To cheer them, great of soul;
And here for all the world to see
They set their Liberty Pole.

O little, blessed, lonely plot
Of our ancestral earth,
What dreams are here as we draw near
The dust that gave us birth!
Out of the ancient mighty dark
These Pilgrims not in vain
Proclaimed the good they saw, then turned
To dust and dreams again.

O never say their dreams are dead
Since West and South and North
They sent their breed to prove their creed
In verity and worth.
Across the conquered leagues that lie
Beneath their dauntless will,
From tent and shack the trails run back
To the foot of Burial Hill.

Slowly we mount the wooded crest,
And there in golden gloom
Stands simple, square, and unadorned,
Our grandsire's altar tomb.
Upon its dark gray slated top
The long inscription reads,
In stately phrase his townsmen's praise
Of his deserts and deeds.

Their "pastor of the Church of Christ,"
They wish the world to feel
The "luster" of his ministry,
His "meekness" and his "zeal."
I doubt not he deserved it all,
And not a word of ill;
For they were just, these men whose dust
Lies here on Burial Hill.

Perhaps we wear the very guise
And features that he wore,
And with the look of his own eyes
Behold his world once more.
Would that his spirit too might live,
While lives his goodly name,
To move among the sons of men,
"A minister of flame."

So might his magic gift of words,
Not wholly passed away,
Survive to be a sorcery
In all men's hearts to-day,
To plead no less for loveliness
Than truth and goodness still.
God rest you, sir, his minister,
Asleep on Burial Hill!

THE WISE MEN FROM THE EAST

"Why were the Wise Men three,
Instead of five or seven?"
They had to match, you see,
The archangels in Heaven.

God sent them, sure and swift,
By his mysterious presage,
To bear the threefold gift
And take the threefold message.

Thus in their hands were seen
The gold of purest Beauty,
The myrrh of Truth all-clean,
The frankincense of Duty.

And thus they bore away
The loving heart's great treasure,
And knowledge clear as day,
To be our life's new measure.

They went back to the East
To spread the news of gladness.
There one became a priest
Of the new word to sadness;

And one a workman, skilled

Beyond the old earth's fashion;
And one a scholar, filled
With learning's endless passion.

God sent them for a sign
He would not change nor alter
His good and fair design,
However man may falter.

He meant that, as He chose
His perfect plan and willed it,
They stood in place of those
Who elsewhere had fulfilled it;

Whoso would mark and reach
The height of man's election,
Must still achieve and teach
The triplicate perfection.

For since the world was made,
One thing was needed ever,
To keep man undismayed
Through failure and endeavor —

A faultless trinity
Of body, mind, and spirit,
And each with its own three
Strong angels to be near it;

Strength to arise and go
Wherever dawn is breaking,
Poise like the tides that flow,
Instinct for beauty-making;

Imagination bold
To cross the mystic border,
Reason to seek and hold,
Judgment for law and order;

Joy that makes all things well,
Faith that is all-availing
Each terror to dispel,
And Love, ah, Love unfailing.

These are the flaming Nine
Who walk the world unsleeping,
Sent forth by the Divine
With manhood in their keeping.

These are the seraphs strong
His mighty soul had need of,
When He would right the wrong
And sorrow He took heed of.

And that, I think, is why
The Wise Men knelt before Him,
And put their kingdoms by
To serve Him and adore Him;

So that our Lord, unknown,
Should not be unattended,
When He was here alone
And poor and unbefriended;

That still He might have three
(Rather than five or seven)
To stand in their degree,
Like archangels in Heaven.

A WATER COLOR

There's a picture in my room
Lightens many an hour of gloom, —

Cheers me under fortune's frown
And the drudgery of town.

Many and many a winter day
When my soul sees all things gray,

Here is veritable June,
Heart's content and spirit's boon.

It is scarce a hand-breadth wide,
Not a span from side to side,

Yet it is an open door
Looking back to joy once more,

Where the level marshes lie,
A quiet journey of the eye,

And the unsubstantial blue
Makes the fine illusion true.

So I forth and travel there
In the blessed light and air,

Miles of green tranquillity
Down the river to the sea.

Here the sea-birds roam at will,
And the sea-wind on the hill

Brings the hollow pebbly roar
From the dim and rosy shore,

With the very scent and draft
Of the old sea's mighty craft.

I am standing on the dunes,
By some charm that must be June's,

When the magic of her hand
Lays a sea-spell on the land.

And the old enchantment falls
On the blue-gray orchard walls

And the purple high-top boles,
While the orange orioles

Flame and whistle through the green
Of that paradisal scene.

Strolling idly for an hour
Where the elder is in flower,

I can hear the bob-white call
Down beyond the pasture wall.

Musing in the scented heat,
Where the bayberry is sweet,

I can see the shadows run
Up the cliff-side in the sun.

Or I cross the bridge and reach
The mossers' houses on the beach,

Where the bathers on the sand
Lie sea-freshened and sun-tanned.

Thus I pass the gates of time
And the boundaries of clime,

Change the ugly man-made street
For God's country green and sweet.

Fag of body, irk of mind,
In a moment left behind,

Once more I possess my soul
With the poise and self-control

Beauty gives the free of heart
Through the sorcery of art,

EL DORADO

This is the story
Of Santo Domingo,
The first established
Permanent city
Built in the New World.
Miguel Dias,
A Spanish sailor
In the fleet of Columbus,
Fought with a captain,
Wounded him, then in fear
Fled from his punishment.

Ranging the wilds, he came
On a secluded
Indian village
Of the peace-loving
Comely Caguisas.
There he found shelter,
Food, fire, and hiding, —
Welcome unstinted.

Over this tribe ruled —
No cunning chieftain
Grown gray in world-craft,
But a young soft-eyed
Girl, tender-hearted,
Loving, and regal
Only in beauty,

With no suspicion
Of the perfidious
Merciless gold-lust
Of the white sea-wolves, —
Roving, rapacious,
Conquerors, destroyers.
Strongly the stranger
Wooed with his foreign
Manners, his Latin
Fervor and graces;
Beat down her gentle
Unreserved strangeness;

Made himself consort
Of a young queen, all
Loveliness, ardor,
And generous devotion.
Her world she gave him,
Nothing denied him,
All, all for love's sake
Poured out before him, —
Lived but to pleasure
And worship her lover.

Such is the way
Of free-hearted women,
Radiant beings
Who carry God's secret;
All their seraphic
Unworldly wisdom
Spent without fearing
Or calculation
For the enrichment
Of — whom, what, and wherefore?

Ask why the sun shines
And is not measured,
Ask why the rain falls
Aeon by aeon,
Ask why the wind comes
Making the strong trees
Blossom in springtime,
Forever unwearied!
Whoever earned these gifts,
Air, sun, and water?
Whoever earned his share
In that unfathomed
Full benediction,

Passing the old earth's
Cunningest knowledge,
Greater than all
The ambition of ages,
Light as a thistle-seed,
Strong as a tide-run,
Vast and mysterious
As the night sky, —
The love of woman?

Not long did Miguel
Dias abide content
With his good fortune.
Back to his voyaging
Turned his desire,
Restless once more to rove
With boon companions,
Filled with the covetous
Thirst for adventure, —
The white man's folly.

Then poor Zamcaca,
In consternation
Lest she lack merit
Worthy to tether
His wayward fancy,
Knowing no way but love,
Guileless, and sedulous
Only to gladden,
Quick and sweet-souled
As another madonna,
Gave him the secret
Of her realm's treasure, —
Raw gold unweighed,
Stored wealth unimagined;
Decked him with trappings
Of that yellow peril;
And bade him go
Bring his comrades to settle
In her dominion.

Not long the Spaniards
Stood on that bidding.
Gold was their madness,
Their Siren and Pandar.
Trooping they followed
Their friend the explorer,

Greed-fevered ravagers
Of all things goodly,
Hot-foot to plunder
The land of his love-dream.
They swooped on that country,
Founded their city,
Made Miguel Dias
Its first Alcalde, —
Flattered and fooled him,
Loud in false praises
For the great wealth he had
By his love's bounty.

Then the old story,
Older than Adam, —
Treachery, rapine,
Ingratitude, bloodshed,
Wrought by the strong man
On unsuspecting
And gentler brothers.
The rabid Spaniard,
Christian and ruthless
(Like any modern
Magnate of Mammon),
Harried that fearless,
Light-hearted, trustful folk
Under his booted heel.
Tears (ah, a woman's tears, —
The grief of angels, —)
Fell from Zamcaca,
Sorrowing, hopeless,
Alone, for her people.

Sick from injustice,
Distraught, and disheartened,
Tortured by sight and sound
Of wrong and ruin,
When the kind, silent,
Tropical moonlight,
Lay on the city,
In the dead hour
When the soul trembles
Within the portals
Of its own province,
While far away seem
All deeds of daytime,
She rose and wondered;
Gazed on the sleeping

Face of her loved one,
Alien and cruel;
Kissed her strange children,
Longingly laying a hand
In farewell on each,
Crept to the door, and fled
Back to the forest.

Only the deep heart
Of the World-mother,
Brooding below the storms
Of human madness,
Can know what desolate
Anguish possessed her.

Only the far mind
Of the World-father,
Seeing the mystic
End and beginning,
Knows why the pageant
Is so betattered
With mortal sorrow.

A PAINTER'S HOLIDAY

We painters sometimes strangely keep
These holidays. When life runs deep
And broad and strong, it comes to make
Its own bright-colored almanack.
Impulse and incident divine
Must find their way through tone and line;
The throb of color and the dream
Of beauty, giving art its theme
From dear life's daily miracle,
Illume the artist's life as well.
A bird-note, or a turning leaf,
The first white fall of snow, a brief
Wild song from the Anthology,
A smile, or a girl's kindling eye, —
And there is worth enough for him
To make the page of history dim.
Who knows upon what day may come
The touch of that delirium
Which lifts plain life to the divine,
And teaches hand the magic line
No cunning rule could ever reach,

Where Soul's necessities find speech?
None knows how rapture may arrive
To be our helper, and survive
Through our essay to help in turn
All starving eager souls who yearn
Lightward discouraged and distraught.
Ah, once art's gleam of glory caught
And treasured in the heart, how then
We walk enchanted among men,
And with the elder gods confer!
So art is hope's interpreter,
And with devotion must conspire
To fan the eternal altar fire.
Wherefore you find me here to-day,
Not idling the good hours away,
But picturing a magic hour
With its replenishment of power.

Conceive a bleak December day,
The streets all mire, the sky all gray,
And a poor painter trudging home
Disconsolate, when what should come
Across his vision, but a line
On a bold-lettered play-house sign,
A Persian Sun Dance.

In he turns.
A step, and there the desert burns
Purple and splendid; molten gold
The streamers of the dawn unfold,
Amber and amethyst uphurled
Above the far rim of the world;
The long-held sound of temple bells
Over the hot sand steals and swells;
A lazy tom-tom throbs and drones
In barbarous maddening monotones;
While sandal incense blue and keen
Hangs in the air. And then the scene
Wakes, and out steps, by rhythm released,
The sorcery of all the East,
In rose and saffron gossamer, —
A young light-hearted worshipper
Who dances up the sun. She moves
Like waking woodland flower that loves
To greet the day. Her lithe brown curve
Is like a sapling's sway and swerve
Before the spring wind. Her dark hair
Framing a face vivid and rare,

Curled to her throat and then flew wild,
Like shadows round a radiant child.
The sunlight from her cymbals played
About her dancing knees, and made
A world of rose-lit ecstasy,
Prophetic of the day to be.

Such mystic beauty might have shone
In Sardis or in Babylon,
To bring a Satrap to his doom
Or touch some lad with glory's bloom.
And now it wrought for me, with sheer
Enchantment of the dying year,
Its irresistible reprieve
From joylessness on New Year's Eve.

MIRAGE

Here hangs at last, you see, my row
Of sketches, — all I have to show
Of one enchanted summer spent
In sweet laborious content,
At little 'Sconset by the moors,
With the sea thundering by its doors,
Its grassy streets, and gardens gay
With hollyhocks and salvia.

And here upon the easel yet,
With the last brush of paint still wet,
(Showing how inspiration toils),
Is one where the white surf-line boils
Along the sand, and the whole sea
Lifts to the skyline, just to be
The wondrous background from whose verge
Of blue on blue there should emerge
This miracle.

One day of days
I strolled the silent path that strays
Between the moorlands and the beach
From Siasconset, till you reach
Tom Nevers Head, the lone last land
That fronts the ocean, lone and grand
As when the Lord first bade it be
For a surprise and mystery.
A sailless sea, a cloudless sky,

The level lonely moors, and I
The only soul in all that vast
Of color made intense to last!
The small white sea-birds piping near;
The great soft moor-winds; and the dear
Bright sun that pales each crest to jade,
Where gulls glint fishing unafraid.
Here man the godlike might have gone
With his deep thought, on that wild dawn
When the first sun came from the sea,
Glowing and kindling the world to be,
While time began and joy had birth, —
No wilder sweeter spot on earth!

As I sat there and mused (the way
We painters waste our time, you say!)
On the sheer loneliness and strength
Whence life must spring, there came at length
Conviction of the helplessness
Of earth alone to ban or bless.
I saw the huge unhuman sea;
I heard the drear monotony
Of the waves beating on the shore
With heedless, futile strife and roar,
Without a meaning or an aim.
And then a revelation came,
In subtle, sudden, lovely guise,
Like one of those soft mysteries
Of Indian jugglers, who evoke
A flower for you out of smoke.
I knew sheer beauty without soul
Could never be perfection's goal,
Nor satisfy the seeking mind
With all it longs for and must find
One day. The lovely things that haunt
Our senses with an aching want,
And move our souls, are like the fair
Lost garments of a soul somewhere.
Nature is naught, if not the veil
Of some great good that must prevail
And break in joy, as woods of spring
Break into song and blossoming.
But what makes that great goodness start
Within ourselves? When leaps the heart
With gladness, only then we know
Why lovely Nature travails so, —
Why art must persevere and pray
In her incomparable way.

In all the world the only worth
Is human happiness; its dearth
The darkest ill. Let joyance be,
And there is God's sufficiency, —
Such joy as only can abound
Where the heart's comrade has been found.

That was my thought. And then the sea
Broke in upon my revery
With clamorous beauty, — the superb
Eternal noun that takes no verb
But love. The heaven of dove-like blue
Bent o'er the azure, round and true
As magic sphere of crystal glass,
Where faith sees plain the pageant pass
Of things unseen. So I beheld
The sheer sky-arches domed and belled,
As if the sea were the very floor
Of heaven where walked the gods of yore
In Plato's imagery, and I
Uplifted saw their pomps go by.

The House of space and time grew tense
As if with rapture's imminence,
When truth should be at last made clear,
And the great worth of life appear;
While I, a worshipper at the shrine,
For very longing grew divine,
Borne upward on earth's ecstasy,
And welcomed by the boundless sky.
A mighty prescience seemed to brood
Over that tenuous solitude
Yearning for form, till it became
Vivid as dream and live as flame,
Through magic art could never match,
The vision I have tried to catch, —
All earth's delight and meaning grown
A lyric presence loved and known.

How otherwise could time evolve
Young courage, or the high resolve,
Or gladness to assuage and bless
The soul's austere great loneliness,
Than by providing her somehow
With sympathy of hand and brow,
And bidding her at last go free,
Companioned through eternity?

So there appeared before my eyes,
In a beloved familiar guise,
A vivid questing human face
In profile, scanning heaven for grace,
Up-gazing there against the blue
With eyes that heaven itself shone through;
The lips soft-parted, half in prayer,
Half confident of kindness there;
A brow like Plato's made for dream
In some immortal Academe,
And tender as a happy girl's;
A full dark head of clustered curls
Round as an emperor's, where meet
Repose and ardor, strong and sweet,
Distilling from a mind unmarred
The glory of her rapt regard.
So eager Mary might have stood,
In love's adoring attitude,
And looked into the angel's eyes
With faith and fearlessness, all wise
In soul's unfaltering innocence,
Sure in her woman's supersense
Of things only the humble know.
My vision looks forever so.

In other years when men shall say,
"What was the painter's meaning, pray?
Why all this vast of sea and space,
Just to enframe a woman's face?"
Here is the pertinent reply,
"What better use for earth and sky?"

The great archangel passed that way
Illuming life with mystic ray.
Not Lippo's self nor Raphael
Had lovelier realer things to tell
Than I, beholding far away
How all the melting rose and gray
Upon the purple sea-line leaned
About that head that intervened.

How real was she? Ah, my friend,
In art the fact and fancy blend
Past telling. All the painter's task
Is with the glory. Need we ask
The tulips breaking through the mould
To their untarnished age of gold,
Whence their ideals were derived

That have so gloriously survived?
Flowers and painters both must give
The hint they have received, to live, —
Spend without stint the joy and power
That lurk in each propitious hour, —
Yet leave the why untold — God's way.
My sketch is all I have to say.

THE WINGED VICTORY

Thou dear and most high Victory,
Whose home is the unvanquished sea,
Whose fluttering wind-blown garments keep.
The very freshness, fold, and sweep
They wore upon the galley's prow,
By what unwonted favor now
Hast thou alighted in this place,
Thou Victory of Samothrace?

O thou to whom in countless lands
With eager hearts and striving hands
Strong men in their last need have prayed,
Greatly desiring, undismayed,
And thou hast been across the fight
Their consolation and their might,
Withhold not now one dearer grace,
Thou Victory of Samothrace!

Behold, we too must cry to thee,
Who wage our strife with Destiny,
And give for Beauty and for Truth
Our love, our valor and our youth.
Are there no honors for these things
To match the pageantries of kings?
Are we more laggard in the race
Than those who fell at Samothrace?

Not only for the bow and sword,
O Victory, be thy reward!
The hands that work with paint and clay
In Beauty's service, shall not they
Also with mighty faith prevail?
Let hope not die, nor courage fail,
But joy come with thee pace for pace,
As once long since in Samothrace.

Grant us the skill to shape the form
And spread the color living-warm,
(As they who wrought aforetime did),
Where love and wisdom shall lie hid,
In fair impassioned types, to sway
The cohorts of the world to-day,
In Truth's eternal cause, and trace
Thy glory down from Samothrace.

With all the ease and splendid poise
Of one who triumphs without noise,
Wilt thou not teach us to attain
Thy sense of power without strain,
That we a little may possess
Our souls with thy sure loveliness, —
That calm the years cannot deface,
Thou Victory of Samothrace?

Then in the ancient ceaseless war
With infamy, go thou before!
Amid the shoutings and the drums
Let it be learned that Beauty comes,
Man's matchless Paladin to be,
Whose rule shall make his spirit free
As thine from all things mean or base,
Thou Victory of Samothrace.

TRIUMPHALIS

Soul, art thou sad again
With the old sadness?
Thou shalt be glad again
With a new gladness,
When April sun and rain
Mount to the teeming brain
With the earth madness.

When from the mould again,
Spurning disaster,
Spring shoots unfold again,
Follow thou faster
Out of the drear domain
Of dark, defeat, and pain,
Praising the Master.

Light for thy guide again,

Ample and splendid;
Love at thy side again,
All doubting ended;
(Ah, by the dragon slain,
For nothing small or vain
Michael contended!)

Thou shalt take heart again,
No more despairing;
Play thy great part again,
Loving and caring.
Hark how the gold refrain
Runs through the iron strain,
Splendidly daring!

Thou shalt grow strong again,
Confident, tender, —
Battle with wrong again,

Be truth's defender, —
Of the immortal train,
Born to attempt, attain,
Never surrender!

THE ENCHANTED TRAVELLER

We travelled empty-handed
With hearts all fear above,
For we ate the bread of friendship,
We drank the wine of love.

Through many a wondrous autumn,
Through many a magic spring,
We hailed the scarlet banners,
We heard the blue-bird sing.

We looked on life and nature
With the eager eyes of youth,
And all we asked or cared for
Was beauty, joy, and truth.

We found no other wisdom,
We learned no other way,
Than the gladness of the morning,
The glory of the day.

So all our earthly treasure
Shall go with us, my dears,
Aboard the Shadow Liner,
Across the sea of years.

Bliss Carman - An Appreciation

How many Canadians—how many even among the few who seek to keep themselves informed of the best in contemporary literature, who are ever on the alert for the new voices—realise, or even suspect, that this Northern land of theirs has produced a poet of whom it may be affirmed with confidence and assurance that he is of the great succession of English poets? Yet such—strange and unbelievable though it may seem—is in very truth the case, that poet being (to give him his full name) William Bliss Carman. Canada has full right to be proud of her poets, a small body though they are; but not only does Mr. Carman stand high and clear above them all—his place (and time cannot but confirm and justify the assertion) is among those men whose poetry is the shining glory of that great English literature which is our common heritage.

If any should ask why, if what has been just said is so, there has been—as must be admitted—no general recognition of the fact in the poet's home land, I would answer that there are various and plausible, if not good, reasons for it.

First of all, the poet, as thousands more of our young men of ambition and confidence have done, went early to the United States, and until recently, except for rare and brief visits to his old home down by the sea, has never returned to Canada—though for all that, I am able to state, on his own authority, he is still a Canadian citizen. Then all his books have had their original publication in the United States, and while a few of them have subsequently carried the imprints of Canadian publishers, none of these can be said ever to have made any special effort to push their sale. Another reason for the fact above mentioned is that Mr. Carman has always scorned to advertise himself, while his work has never been the subject of the log-rolling and booming which the work of many another poet has had—to his ultimate loss. A further reason is that he follows a rule of his own in preparing his books for publication. Most poets publish a volume of their work as soon as, through their industry and perseverance, they have material enough on hand to make publication desirable in their eyes. Not so with Mr. Carman, however, his rule being not to publish until he has done sufficient work of a certain general character or key to make a volume. As a result, you cannot fully know or estimate his work by one book, or two books, or even half a dozen; you must possess or be familiar with every one of the score and more volumes which contain his output of poetry before you can realise how great and how many-sided is his genius.

It is a common remark on the part of those who respond readily to the vigorous work of Kipling, or Masefield, even our own Service, that Bliss Carman's poetry has no relation to or concern with ordinary, everyday life. One would suppose that most persons who cared for poetry at all turned to it as a relief from or counter to the burdens and vexations of the daily round; but in any event, the remark referred to seems to me to indicate either the most casual acquaintance with Mr. Carman's work, or a complete misunderstanding and misapprehension of the meaning of it. I grant that you will find little or nothing in it all to remind you of the grim realities and vexing social problems of this modern existence of ours; but to say or to suggest that these things do not exist for Mr. Carman is to say or to suggest something which is the reverse of true. The truth is, he is aware of them as only one with the sensitive organism of a poet can be; but he does not feel that he has a call or mission to remedy them, and still less to sing of them. He therefore leaves the immediate problems of the day to those who choose, or are led, to occupy themselves therewith, and turns resolutely away to dwell upon those things which for him possess infinitely greater importance.

"What are they?" one who knows Mr. Carman only as, say, a lyrist of spring or as a singer of the delights of vagabondia probably will ask in some wonder. Well, the things which concern him above all, I would answer, are first, and naturally, the beauty and wonder of this world of ours, and next the mystery of the earthly pilgrimage of the human soul out of eternity and back into it again.

The poems in the present volume—which, by the way, can boast the high honor of being the very first regular Canadian edition of his work—will be evidence ample and conclusive to every reader, I am sure, of the place which

The perennial enchanted
Lovely world and all its lore

occupy in the heart and soul of Bliss Carman, as well as of the magical power with which he is able to convey the deep and unfailing satisfaction and delight which they possess for him. They, however, represent his latest period (he has had three well-defined periods), comprising selections from three of his last published volumes: The Rough Rider, Echoes from Vagabondia, and April Airs, together with a number of new poems, and do not show, except here and there and by hints and flashes, how great is his preoccupation with the problem of man's existence—

—the hidden import
Of man's eternal plight.

This is manifest most in certain of his earlier books, for in these he turns and returns to the greatest of all the problems of man almost constantly, probing, with consummate and almost unrivalled use of the art of expression, for the secret which surely, he clearly feels, lies hidden somewhere, to be discovered if one could but pierce deeply enough. Pick up Behind the Arras, and as you turn over page after page you cannot but observe how incessantly the poet's mind—like the minds of his two great masters, Browning and Whitman—works at this problem. In "Behind the Arras," the title poem; "In the Wings," "The Crimson House," "The Lodger," "Beyond the Gamut," "The Juggler"—yes, in every poem in the book—he takes up and handles the strange thing we know as, or call, life, turning it now this way, now that, in an effort to find out its meaning and purpose. He comes but little nearer success in this than do most of the rest of men, of course; but the magical and ever-fresh beauty of his expression, the haunting melody of his lines, the variety of his images and figures and the depth and range of his thought, put his searchings and ponderings in a class by themselves.

Lengthy quotation from Mr. Carman's books is not permitted here, and I must guide myself accordingly, though with reluctance, because I believe that in a study such as this the subject should be allowed to speak for himself as much as possible. In "Behind the Arras" the poet describes the passage from life to death as

A cadence dying down unto its source
In music's course,

and goes on to speak of death as

—the broken rhythm of thought and man,
The sweep and span
Of memory and hope
About the orbit where they still must grope
For wider scope,

To be through thousand springs restored, renewed,
With love imbrued,
With increments of will
Made strong, perceiving unattainment still
From each new skill.

Now follow some verses from "Behind the Gamut," to my mind the poet's greatest single achievement;

As fine sand spread on a disc of silver,
At some chord which bids the motes combine,
Heeding the hidden and reverberant impulse,
Shifts and dances into curve and line,

The round earth, too, haply, like a dust-mote,
Was set whirling her assigned sure way,
Round this little orb of her ecliptic
To some harmony she must obey.

And what of man?

Linked to all his half-accomplished fellows,
Through unfrontiered provinces to range—
Man is but the morning dream of nature,
Roused to some wild cadence weird and strange.

Here, now, are some verses from "Pulvis et Umbra," which is to be found in Mr. Carman's first book, Low
Tide on Grand Pré, and in which the poet addresses a moth which a storm has blown into his window:

For man walks the world with mourning
Down to death and leaves no trace,
With the dust upon his forehead,
And the shadow on his face.

Pillared dust and fleeing shadow
As the roadside wind goes by,
And the fourscore years that vanish
In the twinkling of an eye.

"Pillared dust and fleeing shadow." Where in all our English literature will one find the life history of
man summed up more briefly and, at the same time, more beautifully, than in that wonderful line? Now

follows a companion verse to those just quoted, taken from "Lord of My Heart's Elation," which stands in the forefront of From the Green Book of the Bards. It may be remarked here that while the poet recurs again and again to some favorite thought or idea, it is never in the same words. His expression is always new and fresh, showing how deep and true is his inspiration. Again it is man who is pictured:

A fleet and shadowy column
Of dust and mountain rain,
To walk the earth a moment
And be dissolved again.

But while Mr. Carman's speculations upon life's meaning and the mystery of the future cannot but appeal to the thoughtful-minded, it is as an interpreter of nature that he makes his widest appeal. Bliss Carman, I must say here, and emphatically, is no mere landscape-painter; he never, or scarcely ever, paints a picture of nature for its own sake. He goes beyond the outward aspect of things and interprets or translates for us with less keen senses as only a poet whose feeling for nature is of the deepest and profoundest, who has gone to her whole-heartedly and been taken close to her warm bosom, can do. Is this not evident from these verses from "The Great Return"—originally called "The Pagan's Prayer," and for some inscrutable reason to be found only in the limited Collected Poems, issued in two stately volumes in 1905.

When I have lifted up my heart to thee,
Thou hast ever hearkened and drawn near,
And bowed thy shining face close over me,
Till I could hear thee as the hill-flowers hear.

When I have cried to thee in lonely need,
Being but a child of thine bereft and wrung,
Then all the rivers in the hills gave heed;
And the great hill-winds in thy holy tongue—

That ancient incommunicable speech—
The April stars and autumn sunsets know—
Soothed me and calmed with solace beyond reach
Of human ken, mysterious and low.

Who can read or listen to those moving lines without feeling that Mr. Carman is in very truth a poet of nature—nay, Nature's own poet? But how could he be other when, in "The Breath of the Reed" (From the Green Book of the Bards), he makes the appeal?

Make me thy priest, O Mother,
And prophet of thy mood,
With all the forest wonder
Enraptured and imbued.

As becomes such a poet, and particularly a poet whose birth-month is April, Mr. Carman sings much of the early spring. Again and again he takes up his woodland pipe, and lo! Pan himself and all his train troop joyously before us. Yet the singer's notes for all his singing never become wearied or strident; his airs are ever new and fresh; his latest songs are no less spontaneous and winning than were his first, written how many years ago, while at the same time they have gained in beauty and melody. What heart will not stir to the vibrant music of his immortal "Spring Song," which was originally published in the first Songs from Vagabondia, and the opening verses of which follow?

Make me over, mother April,
When the sap begins to stir!
When thy flowery hand delivers
All the mountain-prisoned rivers,
And thy great heart beats and quivers
To revive the days that were,
Make me over, mother April,
When the sap begins to stir!

Take my dust and all my dreaming,
Count my heart-beats one by one,
Send them where the winters perish;
Then some golden noon recherish
And restore them in the sun,
Flower and scent and dust and dreaming,
With their heart-beats every one!

That poem is sufficient in itself to prove that Bliss Carman has full right and title to be called Spring's own lyrist, though it may be remarked here that not all his spring poems are so unfeignedly joyous. Many of them indeed, have a touch, or more than a touch, of wistfulness, for the poet knows well that sorrow lurks under all joy, deep and well hidden though it may be.

Mr. Carman sings equally finely, though perhaps not so frequently, of summer and the other seasons; but as he has other claims upon our attention, I shall forbear to labor the fact, particularly as the following collection demonstrates it sufficiently. One of those other claims is as a writer of sea poetry. Few poets, it may be said, have pictured the majesty and the mystery, the beauty and the terror of the sea, better than he. His Ballads of Lost Haven is a veritable treasure-house for those whose spirits find kinship in wide expanses of moving waters. One of the best known poems in this volume is "The Gravedigger," which opens thus:

Oh, the shambling sea is a sexton old,
And well his work is done.
With an equal grave for lord and knave,
He buries them every one.

Then hoy and rip, with a rolling hip,
He makes for the nearest shore;
And God, who sent him a thousand ship,
Will send him a thousand more;
But some he'll save for a bleaching grave,
And shoulder them in to shore—
Shoulder them in, shoulder them in,
Shoulder them in to shore.

In "The City of the Sea" (Last Songs from Vagabondia) Mr. Carman speaks of the seabells sounding

The eternal cadence of sea sorrow
For Man's lot and immemorial wrong—
The lost strains that haunt the human dwelling
With the ghost of song.

Elsewhere he speaks of

The great sea, mystic and musical.

And here from another poem is a striking picture:

... the old sea
Seems to whimper and deplore
Mourning like a childless crone
With her sorrow left alone—
The eternal human cry
To the heedless passer-by.

I have said above that Mr. Carman has had three distinct periods, and intimated that the poems in the following collection are of his third period. The first period may be said to be represented by the Low Tide and Behind the Arras volumes, while the second is displayed in the three volumes of Songs from Vagabondia, which he published in association with his friend Richard Hovey. Bliss Carman was from the first too original and individual a poet to be directly influenced by anyone else; but there can be no doubt that his friendship with Hovey helped to turn him from over-preoccupation with mysteries which, for all their greatness, are not for man to solve, to an intenser realisation of the beauty and loveliness of the world about him and of the joys of human fellowship. The result is seen in such poems as "Spring Song," quoted in part above, and his perhaps equally well-known "The Joys of the Road," which appeared in the same volume with that poem, and a few verses from which follow:

Now the joys of the road are chiefly these:
A crimson touch on the hardwood trees;

A vagrant's morning wide and blue,
In early fall, when the wind walks, too;

A shadowy highway cool and brown,
Alluring up and enticing down

From rippled waters and dappled swamp,
From purple glory to scarlet pomp;

The outward eye, the quiet will,
And the striding heart from hill to hill.

Some of the finest of arman's work is contained in his elegiac or memorial poems, in which he commemorates Keats, Shelley, William Blake, Lincoln, Stevenson, and other men for whom he has a kindred feeling, and also friends whom he has loved and lost. Listen to these moving lines from "Non Omnis Moriar," written in memory of Gleeson White, and to be found in Last Songs from Vagabondia:

There is a part of me that knows,
Beneath incertitude and fear,
I shall not perish when I pass
Beyond mortality's frontier;

But greatly having joyed and grieved,
Greatly content, shall hear the sigh
Of the strange wind across the lone
Bright lands of taciturnity.

In patience therefore I await
My friend's unchanged benign regard,—
Some April when I too shall be
Spilt water from a broken shard.

In "The White Gull," written for the centenary of the birth of Shelley in 1892, and included in By the Aurelian Wall, he thus apostrophizes that clear and shining spirit:

O captain of the rebel host,
Lead forth and far!
Thy toiling troopers of the night
Press on the unavailing fight;
The sombre field is not yet lost,
With thee for star.

Thy lips have set the hail and haste
Of clarions free
To bugle down the wintry verge
Of time forever, where the surge
Thunders and trembles on a waste
And open sea.

In "A Seamark," a threnody for Robert Louis Stevenson, which appears in the same volume, the poet hails "R.L.S." (of whose tribe he may be said to be truly one) as

The master of the roving kind,

and goes on:

O all you hearts about the world
In whom the truant gypsy blood,
Under the frost of this pale time,
Sleeps like the daring sap and flood
That dreams of April and reprieve!
You whom the haunted vision drives,

Incredulous of home and ease.
Perfection's lovers all your lives!

You whom the wander-spirit loves
To lead by some forgotten clue
Forever vanishing beyond
Horizon brinks forever new;
Our restless loved adventurer,
On secret orders come to him,
Has slipped his cable, cleared the reef,
And melted on the white sea-rim.

"Perfection's lovers all your lives." Of these, it may be said without qualification, is Bliss Carman himself.

No summary of Mr. Carman's work, however cursory, would be worthy of the name if it omitted mention of his ventures in the realm of Greek myth. From the Book of Myths is made up of work of that sort, every poem in it being full of the beauty of phrase and melody of which Mr. Carman alone has the secret. The finest poems in the book, barring the opening one, "Overlord," are "Daphne," "The Dead Faun," "Hylas," and "At Phædra's Tomb," but I can do no more here than name them, for extracts would fail to reveal their full beauty. And beauty, after all is said, is the first and last thing with Mr. Carman. As he says himself somewhere:

The joy of the hand that hews for beauty
Is the dearest solace under the sun.

And again

The eternal slaves of beauty
Are the masters of the world.

A slave—a happy, willing slave—to beauty is the poet himself, and the world can never repay him for the message of beauty which he has brought it.

Kindred to From the Book of Myths, but much more important, is Sappho: One Hundred Lyrics, one of the most successful of the numerous attempts which have been made to recapture the poems by that high priestess of song which remain to us only in fragments. Mr. Carman, as Charles G. D. Roberts points out in an introduction to the volume, has made no attempt here at translation or paraphrasing; his venture has been "the most perilous and most alluring in the whole field of poetry"—that of imaginative and, at the same time, interpretive construction. Brief quotation again would fail to convey an adequate idea of the exquisiteness of the work, and all I can do, therefore, is to urge all lovers of real poetry to possess themselves of Sappho: One Hundred Lyrics, for it is literally a storehouse of lyric beauty.

I must not fail here to speak of From the Book of Valentines, which contains some lovely things, notably "At the Great Release." This is not only one of the finest of all Mr. Carman's poems, but it is also one of the finest poems of our time. It is a love poem, and no one possessing any real feeling for poetry can read it without experiencing that strange thrill of the spirit which only the highest form of poetry can communicate. "Morning and Evening," "In an Iris Meadow," and "A letter from Lesbos" must be also mentioned. In the last named poem, Sappho is represented as writing to Gorgo, and expresses herself in these moving words:

If the high gods in that triumphant time
Have calendared no day for thee to come
Light-hearted to this doorway as of old,
Unmoved I shall behold their pomps go by—
The painted seasons in their pageantry,
The silvery progressions of the moon,
And all their infinite ardors unsubdued,
Pass with the wind replenishing the earth

Incredulous forever I must live
And, once thy lover, without joy behold,
The gradual uncounted years go by,
Sharing the bitterness of all things made.

Mention must be now made of Songs of the Sea Children, which can be described only as a collection of the sweetest and tenderest love lyrics written in our time—

—the lyric songs
The earthborn children sing,
When wild-wood laughter throngs
The shy bird-throats of spring;
When there's not a joy of the heart
But flies like a flag unfurled,
And the swelling buds bring back
The April of the world.

So perfect and complete are these lyrics that it would be almost sacrilege to quote any of them unless entire. Listen however, to these verses:

The day is lost without thee,
The night has not a star.
Thy going is an empty room
Whose door is left ajar.

Depart: it is the footfall
Of twilight on the hills.
Return: and every rood of ground
Breaks into daffodils.

There are those who will have it that Bliss Carman has been away from Canada so long that he has ceased to be, in a real sense, a Canadian. Such assume rather than know, for a very little study of his work would show them that it is shot through and through with the poet's feeling for the land of his birth. Memories of his childhood and youthful years down by the sea are still fresh in Mr. Carman's mind, and inspire him again and again in his writing. "A Remembrance," at the beginning of the present collection, may be pointed to as a striking instance of this, but proof positive is the volume, Songs from a

Northern Garden, for it could have been written only by a Canadian, born and bred, one whose heart and soul thrill to the thought of Canada. I would single out from this volume for special mention as being "Canadian" in the fullest sense "In a Grand Pré Garden," "The Keeper's Silence," "At Home and Abroad," "Killoleet," and "Above the Gaspereau," but have no space to quote from them.

But Mr. Carman is not only a Canadian, he is also a Briton; and evidence of this is his Ode on the Coronation, written on the occasion of the crowning of King Edward VII in 1902. This poem—the very existence of which is hardly known among us—ought to be put in the hands of every child and youth who speaks the English tongue, for no other, I dare maintain—nothing by Kipling, or Newbolt, or any other of our so-called "Imperial singers"—expresses more truly and more movingly the deep feeling of love and reverence which the very thought of England evokes in every son of hers, even though it may never have been his to see her white cliffs rise or to tread her storied ground:

O England, little mother by the sleepless Northern tide,
Having bred so many nations to devotion, trust, and pride,
Very tenderly we turn
With welling hearts that yearn
Still to love you and defend you,—let the sons of men discern
Wherein your right and title, might and majesty, reside.

In concluding this, I greatly fear, lamentably inadequate study, I come to the collection which follows, and which, as intimated above, represents the work of Mr. Carman's latest period. I must say at once that, while I yield to no one in admiration for Low Tide and the other books of that period, or for the work of the second period, as represented by the Songs from Vagabondia volumes, I have no hesitation in declaring that I regard the poet's work of the past few years with even higher admiration. It may not possess the force and vigor of the work which preceded it; but anything seemingly missing in that respect is more than made up for me by increased beauty and clarity of expression. The mysticism—verging, or more than verging, at times on symbolism—which marked his earlier poems, and which hung, as it were, as a veil between them and the reader, has gone, and the poet's thought or theme now lies clearly before us as in a mirror. What—to take a verse from the following pages at random—could be more pellucid, more crystal clear in expression—what indeed, could come closer to that achieving of the impossible at which every real poet must aim—than this from "In Gold Lacquer".

Gold are the great trees overhead,
And gold the leaf-strewn grass,
As though a cloth of gold were spread
To let a seraph pass.
And where the pageant should go by,
Meadow and wood and stream,
The world is all of lacquered gold,
Expectant as a dream.

The poet, happily, has fully recovered from the serious illness which laid him low some two years ago, and which for a time caused his friends and admirers the gravest concern, and so we may look forward hopefully to seeing further volumes of verse come from the press to make certain his name and fame. But if, for any reason, this should not be—which the gods forfend!—Later Poems, I dare affirm, must and will be regarded as the fine flower and crowning achievement of the genius and art of Bliss Carman.

R. H. HATHAWAY.
Toronto, 1921.

Bliss Carman – A Short Biography

William Bliss Carman was born in Fredericton, in New Brunswick on April 15th 1861. 'Bliss' was his mother's maiden name. She was descended from Daniel Bliss of Concord, Massachusetts, who was the great-grandfather to Ralph Waldo Emerson.

Carman was educated at Fredericton Collegiate School. Here, under the influence of the headmaster George Robert Parkin, he gained an appreciation of classical literature and was introduced to the poetry of many of the Pre-Raphaelites especially Dante Gabriel Rossetti and Algernon Charles Swinburne.

From here he graduated to the University of New Brunswick, obtaining his B.A. there in 1881. As is common with so many writers his first published piece was for the University magazine and for Carman that was in 1879.

England now beckoned and he spent a year at Oxford and then the University of Edinburgh (1882–1883). He returned home to Canada to work on his M.A. which he obtained from the University of New Brunswick in 1884.

Tragically his father died in January, 1885, followed by his mother in February of the following year. Carman now enrolled in Harvard University for a year. There he met and was part of a literary circle that included the American poet Richard Hovey, who would become his close friend, and later collaborator, on the successful Vagabondia poetry series. Carman and Hovey were members of the "Visionists" circle along with Herbert Copeland and F. Holland Day, who would later form the Boston publishing firm Copeland & Day and, in turn, launch Vagabondia.

After Harvard Carman briefly returned to Canada, but was back in Boston by February of 1890 saying "Boston is one of the few places where my critical education and tastes could be of any use to me in earning money. New York and London are about the only other places." However, he was unable to find work in Boston but was more successful in New York becoming the literary editor of the semi-religious New York Independent. There he helped Canadian poets get published and introduced them to a wider readership than they could receive in Canada.

However, Carman and work as an editor were not destined for a long career together and he was dismissed in 1892. There followed short stays with Current Literature, Cosmopolitan, The Chap-Book, and The Atlantic Monthly. Whilst these appointments provided the basis for a career and an income he was not suited to their demands. From 1895 he would only work as a contributor to magazines and newspapers whilst he worked on his volumes of poetry.

Carman first published a book of poetry in 1893 with Low Tide on Grand Pré. He had written the title poem in the summer of 1886 and it had (whilst he was still at Harvard) been published in the spring of 1887 by Atlantic Monthly. Despite its critical acceptance there was no Canadian company prepared to publish the volume. When an American company did so it went bankrupt. Life was becoming difficult for the young poet.

The following year was decidedly better. His partnership with Richard Hovey had given birth to Songs of Vagabondia and it was published by their friends at Copeland & Day. It was an immediate success. The young men were delighted at such a reception. It quickly sold out and was re-printed a number of times. Although these re-prints were small (usually 500-1000 copies) they were frequent.

On the back of this success they would write a further three volumes, which in their turn were almost as successful. They quickly became the center of a cult following, especially among students who empathized with the poetry's anti-materialistic themes, its celebration of personal freedom, and its glorification of comradeship."

The success of Songs of Vagabondia prompted the Boston firm, Stone & Kimball, to reissue Low Tide on Grand Pré and to hire Carman as the editor of its literary journal, The Chapbook. This ceased after a year when the company relocated and Carman expressed his desire to remain in Boston.

In 1885 Carman brought out Behind the Arras, a somewhat more serious and philosophical work centered on the premise of a long meditation using the speaker's house and its many rooms as a symbol of life and the choices to be made. However, the idea and its execution did not quite meld.

Signficantly, in 1896, Carman met Mrs Mary Perry King, who rapidly became patron, adviser and sometime lover. She put money in his pocket, and food in his mouth and, when he struck bottom, often repaired his confidence as well as helping to sell the work. She also later became his writing collaborator on two verse dramas.

Mitchell Kennerley, Carman's roommate wrote that, "On the rare occasions they had intimate relations they always advised me of by leaving a bunch of violets — Mary favorite flower — on the pillow of my bed." If her husband, Dr. King, knew of this arrangement he seems not to have objected. He was a great supporter of Carman's career and seemingly his wife's complicated involvement with that.

In 1897 Carman published Ballad of Lost Haven, a collection of poetry about the sea. Its notable poems include the macabre sea shanty, The Gravedigger. The following year, 1898, came By the Aurelian Wall, the title poem itself was an elegy to John Keats and the book a collection of formal elegies.

In 1899 his publisher, Lamson, Wolffe was taken over by the Boston firm of Small, Maynard & Co., who had also acquired the rights to Low Tide on Grand Pré. The copyrights to of his books were now held by one publisher and, in lieu of earnings, Carman took what would ultimately be a disastrous financial stake in the company.

As the century turned Carman was hard at work on what would eventually be a five-volume set of poetry; "Pans Pipes". Pan, the goat-god, was traditionally associated with poetry and the coming together of the earthly and the divine. The five volumes were all published between 1902 – 1905.

The inspiration for this came from Mary who had persuaded Carman to write in both prose and poetry about the ideas of 'unitrinianism.' This drew on the theories of François-Alexandre-Nicolas-Chéri Delsarte and was defined as a strategy of mind-body-spirit harmonization aimed at undoing the physical, psychological, and spiritual damage caused by urban modernity. The definition may be rather woolly but for Carman it resulted in some very fine work across the five-volume series. This shared belief between Mary and Carman created a further bond but did isolate him from his circle of friends.

The excellence of a number of these poems did much to install Carman as the most noted of Canadian Poets and eventually their own Poet Laureate. Among the most often quoted and printed are "The Dead Faun" (from Volume I), "Lord of My Heart's Elation" (Volume II) and many of the erotic poems from Volume III.

In the middle of publication in 1903, Small, Maynard failed and with it went all the assets Carman had tied up in the company.

Carman immediately signed with another Boston publisher, L.C. Page, who would publish seven new books of Carman poetry in this hectic period up to 1905. They released a further three books based on Carman's Transcript columns, and a prose work on Unitrinianism, The Making of Personality, that he'd written with Mary King.

Carman now felt secure enough to pursue his 'dream project,' namely a deluxe edition of his collected poetry to 1903. Page acquired the distribution rights on the condition that the book be sold privately, by subscription. Unfortunately, the demand wasn't there and it failed. Carman was deeply disappointed and lost faith in Page. However, their grip on his copyrights was absolute and sadly no further collected editions were to be published during his lifetime.

By 1904 his income was restricted and the offer to be editor-in-chief of the 10-volume project, The World's Best Poetry, was eagerly accepted.

For Carman perhaps his best years as a poet were now behind him. From 1908 he lived near the Kings' New Canaan, Connecticut, estate, that he named "Sunshine", or in the summer in a cabin in the Catskills, which he called "Moonshine."

With Literary tastes now moving away from what he could provide his income further dwindled and his health started to deteriorate.

In 1912 Carman published the final work in the Vagabondia series. Richard Hovey had died in 1900 and so this last work was purely his. It has a distinct elegiac tone as if remembering the past works themselves.

Although Carman was not politically active he did campaign during the World War One, as a member of the Vigilantes, who supported the American entry into the titanic struggle on the Allied side.

By 1920, Carman was impoverished and recovering from a near-fatal attack of tuberculosis. He returned to Canada and began to undertake a series of publicly successful and somewhat lucrative reading tours, saying "there is nothing worth talking of in book sales compared with reading. Breathless attention, crowded halls, and a strange, profound enthusiasm such as I never guessed could be,' he reported to a friend. 'And good thrifty money too. Think of it! An entirely new life for me, and I am the most surprised person in Canada.'"

On October 28th, 1921 Carman was honored at a dinner held by the newly-formed Canadian Authors' Association, at the Ritz Carlton Hotel in Montreal, where he was crowned Canada's Poet Laureate with a wreath of maple leaves.

Carman is placed among the Confederation Poets, a group that included his cousin, Charles G.D. Roberts, Archibald Lampman, and Duncan Campbell Scott. Carman was perhaps the best and is credited with the widest recognition. However, whilst the others carefully supplemented their income with writing novels and works for the magazines, or even other careers, Carman only wrote poetry together with a small amount of writing on literary ideas, philosophy, and aesthetics.

He continued his reading tours, and by 1925 had finally secured a new Canadian publisher; McClelland & Stewart (Toronto), who issued a collection of selected earlier verse and would now became his main publisher. Although they benefited from Carman's increased popularity and his revered position in Canadian literature, his former publisher L.C. Page would not relinquish its copyrights to his earlier works.

In his last years, Carman was a member of the Halifax literary and social set, The Song Fishermen and in 1927 he edited The Oxford Book of American Verse.

William Bliss Carman died of a brain hemorrhage, at the age of 68, in New Canaan on the 8th June, 1929. He was cremated in New Canaan and his ashes interred at Forest Hill Cemetery, Fredericton, with a national memorial service held at the Anglican cathedral there.

It was only a quarter of a century later, on May 13th, 1954, that a scarlet maple tree was planted at his graveside, to honour his request in the 1892 poem "The Grave-Tree":

Let me have a scarlet maple
For the grave-tree at my head,
With the quiet sun behind it,
In the years when I am dead.

Bliss Carman – A Concise Bibliography

Poetry Collections
Low Tide on Grand Pre: A Book of Lyrics (1893)
Songs from Vagabondia (1894)
A Seamark: A Threnody for Robert Louis Stevenson (1895)
Behind the Arras: A Book of the Unseen (1895)
More Songs from Vagabondia (1896)
Ballads of Lost Haven: A Book of the Sea (1897)
By the Aurelian Wall: And Other Elegies (1898)
A Winter Holiday (1899)
Last Songs from Vagabondia (1901)
Ballads and Lyrics (1902)
Ode on the Coronation of King Edward (1902)
Pipes of Pan: From the Book of Myths (1902)
Pipes of Pan: From the Green Book of the Bards (1903)
Pipes of Pan: Songs of the Sea Children (1904)
Pipes of Pan: Songs from a Northern Garden (1904)
Pipes of Pan: From the Book of Valentines (1905)

Sappho: One Hundred Lyrics (1904)
Poems (1905)
The Rough Rider: And Other Poems (1909)
A Painter's Holiday, and Other Poems (1911)
Echoes from Vagabondia (1912)
April Airs: A Book of New England Lyrics (1916)
The Man of The Marne: And Other Poems (1918)
The Vengeance of Noel Brassard: A Tale of the Acadian Expulsion (1919)
Far Horizons (1925)
Later Poems (1926)
Sanctuary: Sunshine House Sonnets (1929)
Wild Garden (1929)
Bliss Carman's Poems (1931)

Drama

Bliss Carman & Mary Perry King. Daughters of Dawn: A Lyrical Pageant of a Series of Historical Scenes for Presentation with Music and Dancing (1913)
Bliss Carman & Mary Perry King. Earth Deities: And Other Rhythmic Masques (1914)

Prose Collections

The Kinship of Nature (1904)
The Poetry of Life (1905)
The Friendship of Art (1908)
The Making of Personality (1908)
Talks on Poetry and Life; Being a Series of Five Lectures Delivered Before the University of Toronto, December 1925 (Speech). transcribed by Blanche Hume. 1926.
Bliss Carman's Scrap-Book: A Table of Contents (Pierce, Lorne, editor) (1931)

Editor

The World's Best Poetry (10 volumes) (1904)
The Oxford Book of American Verse (U.S. editor) (1927)
Carman, Bliss; Pierce, Lorne, editors (1935). Our Canadian Literature: Representative Verse, English and French.